P9-CLS-826

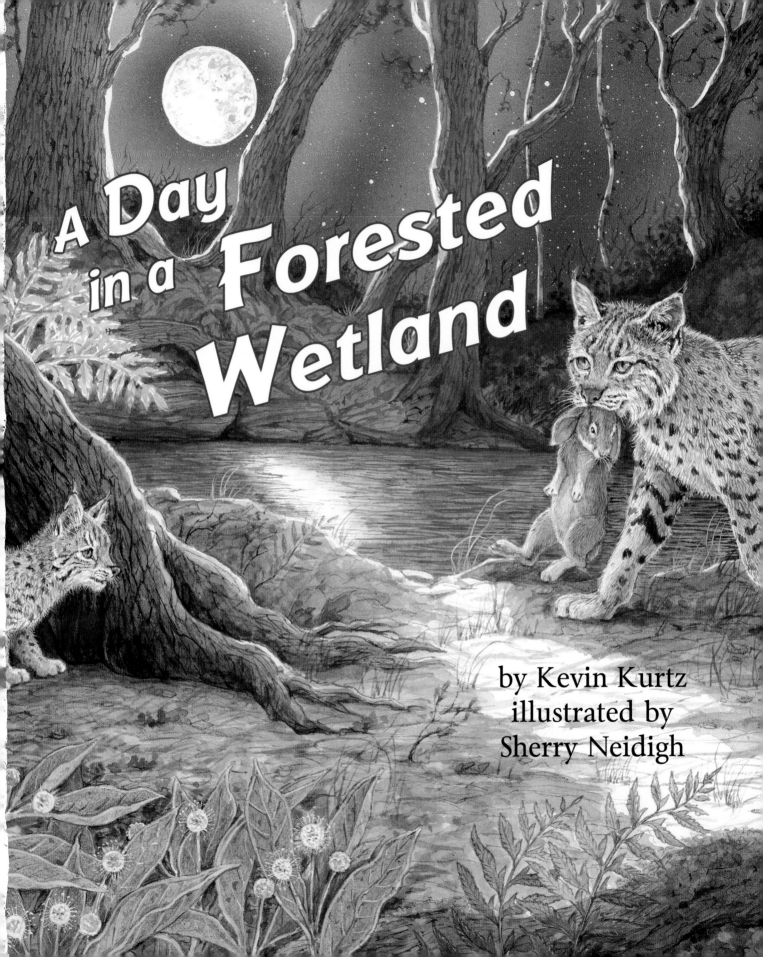

A Day in a Forested Wetland

by Kevin Kurtz

illustrated by Sherry Neidigh

Life in a forested wetland
goes on all day and night.

Some species are active in darkness
while others are active in light.

It's sunrise in the wetland.
A woodpecker flies from a tree.
She just brought her children breakfast.
They never stop feeling hungry.

Look! A wood duck flies at them,
but before their hole is possessed,
the dad chases out the invader
who wanted to steal their nest.

It's morning in the wetland.
A green darner hunts as it flies.
It can see in front and behind it
with its faceted compound eyes.

It spots a nearby mosquito.
Maneuvering around with great flair,
it quickly hones in on the target
and catches its prey in the air.

It's high noon in the wetland.
A turtle in ambush pose
is buried in wetland mud
up to its eyes and its nose.

A snapper can't breathe underwater,
but it has a snorkel to use.
It stretches its neck towards the surface
while its body lies in the ooze.

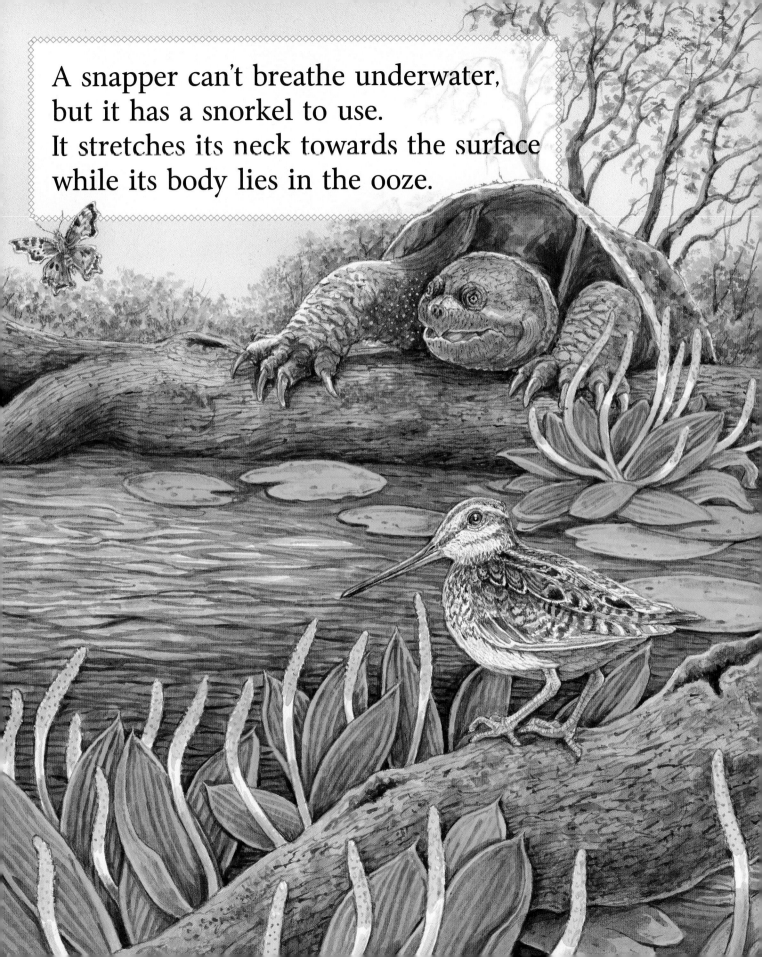

It's afternoon in the wetland.
A caddisfly builds a case
to protect its larval body
from predators in this place.

It uses its silk to fasten
pieces of rocks and plants.
It then can live underwater
while wearing armored pants.

It's sundown in the wetland.
The forest is filled with sound.
Follow it towards the water,
then take a look at the ground.

Camouflaged in leaf litter,
a chorus of frogs awaits.
Sounding like bells that jingle,
spring peepers are calling for mates.

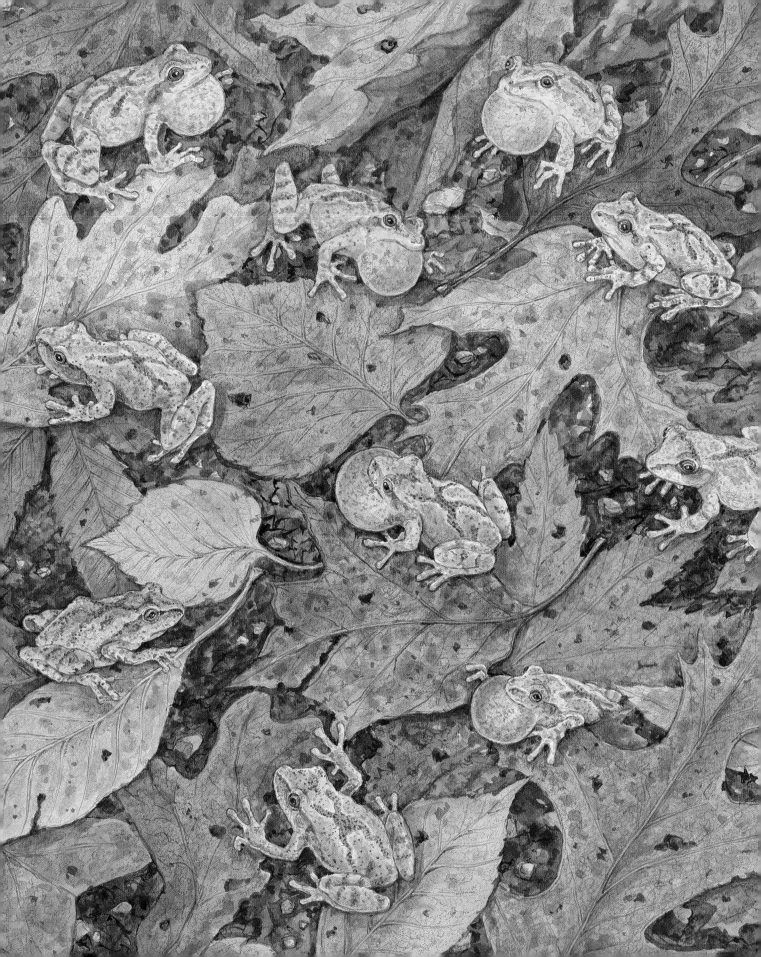

The stars are over the wetland.
Brown bats zig and then zag.
They've eaten their fill of insects
and head back to roost in a snag.

They find their way by listening
to sounds that other bats make.
These noises also will make sure
they don't collide by mistake.

It's midnight in the wetland.
Kittens have just awoke.
They're waiting for their mother,
secure in a hollow oak.

The bobcat quietly approaches.
She knows what her young ones need.
Her hunt was quite successful.
Now it's her children's turn to feed.

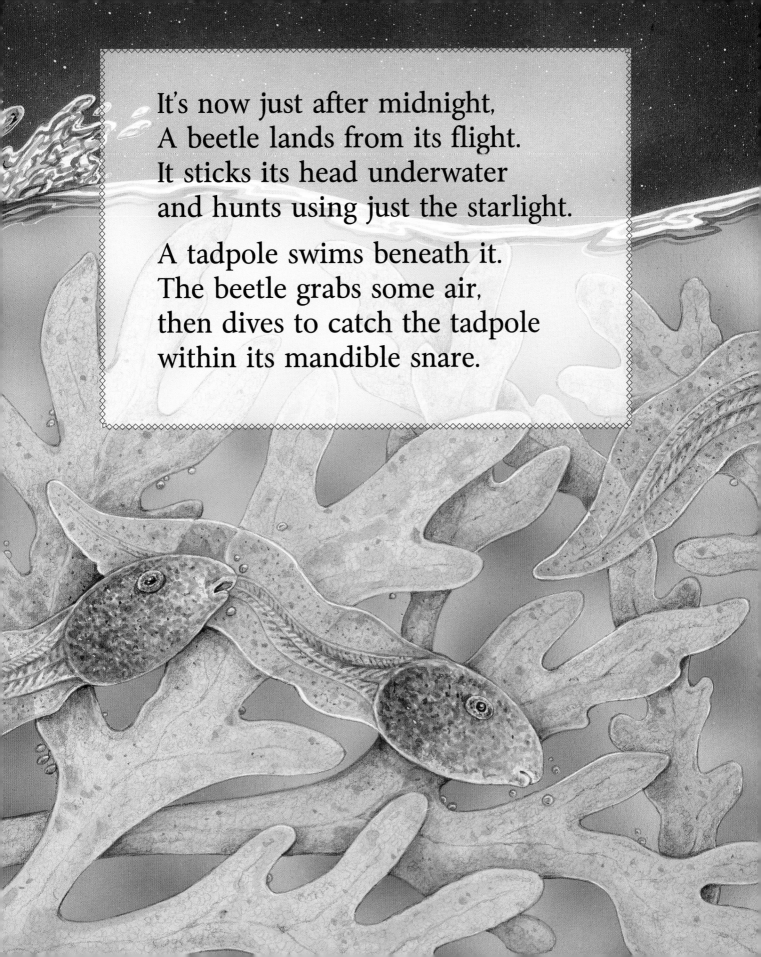

It's now just after midnight,
A beetle lands from its flight.
It sticks its head underwater
and hunts using just the starlight.

A tadpole swims beneath it.
The beetle grabs some air,
then dives to catch the tadpole
within its mandible snare.

It's late night in the wetland.
A squirrel kicks from the bark.
Instead of falling downward,
it glides between trees in the dark.

It lands on a trunk near the swamp bank
and quickly scurries from view.
It's hungry for nuts and mushrooms,
but it must avoid predators too.

Before dawn in the wetland,
on water as black as ink,
a spider sits on the surface
and yet it doesn't sink.

The spider feels a ripple.
It then begins to run
quickly across the surface
until its prey is won.

It's sunrise in the wetland.
An owl flies to the ground.
Though its wings are flapping,
they do not make a sound.

The barred owl wades in water,
and looks for prey to eat.
It spots a tasty crayfish
and grabs it with its feet.

The sun is back on the wetland.
Propped up by its tail,
a beaver gnaws a tree down
with teeth that never fail.

Its dam creates this habitat,
where other species feed
and use this forested wetland
to provide everything they need.

For Creative Minds

This section may be photocopied or printed from our website by the owner of this book for educational, non-commercial use. Cross-curricular teaching activities for use at home or in the classroom, interactive quizzes, and more are available online.

Visit www.ArbordalePublishing.com to explore additional resources.

Keystone Species: Beaver

Beavers are among the few species (including humans) that can make big changes to their environment. This ability to shape their habitat makes beavers into ecosystem engineers.

Beavers shape their environment by building dams. A colony of beavers works together to make a dam out of wood, mud, and stones. The dam slows a stream and creates a pond of still water behind the dam. The pond is usually between three and six feet deep. It helps protect the beavers from land predators like wolves, bears, and coyotes. The pond hides the underwater entrance to the lodge, where the beaver lives.

Beaver dams change a forest into a wetland environment. These changes last for years, even long after the beavers are gone.

In a stone bridge or arch, there is one stone called a keystone. This stone presses down on the others and holds the whole structure in place.

Plants and animals in an ecosystem rely on each other. They help each other meet their basic needs.

Sometimes there is one species that helps support all the other species. This is called a keystone species.

Just like a keystone in an arch holds the structure in place, the keystone species holds the ecosystem in balance. Without the keystone species, the whole ecosystem would suffer.

Beavers are a keystone species. They shape their habitats to create new types of ecosystems, like forested wetlands. Other plants and animals need these new ecosystems.

Beaver Dam Forested Wetland Sequencing

Some forested wetlands are created by beavers. These forested wetlands can last for many years but are not permanent. Put the following stages in order to discover how a beaver makes a forested wetland, and how that forested wetland can change over time.

The answer will spell the word for beavers' genus.

 R   Once the pond completely fills with sediment, it becomes a bog or fen.

 C   A beaver builds a dam across a stream near a forest.

 T   As the forest trees die, more sunlight reaches the pond. Aquatic plants grow.

 O   Over many years, aquatic plants live and die. Old plant matter fills the pond with rich sediment, and the water gets shallower. New marsh plants begin to grow.

 S   Many trees cannot live with their roots underwater. They die in the new forested wetland. Some trees, like alders and cypress, continue to grow and thrive.

 A   The pond behind the dam floods the forest. This creates a forested wetland.

Not all forested wetlands are created by beavers. Some can occur naturally. Forested wetlands can last for centuries, or they may be more temporary habitats. Some forested wetlands are seasonal. They form during spring flooding as water from rain and melted snow overflows rivers and floods low-lying woodlands.

Answer: Castor. The North American beaver belongs to the species *Castor canadensis*.

Wetlands

A wetland is an environment where the soil becomes completely saturated with water. Shallow water sometimes covers the surface for at least part of the year. Wetlands can occur in areas with poor drainage or where the water table is close to the soil surface.

There are four main types of wetlands: forested wetlands (sometimes called swamps), marshes, bogs, and fens. Often multiple types of wetlands can exist side-by-side, without clear barriers between the different types.

As a forested wetland created by a beaver dam changes over time, it can become which of these other wetland types?

What do forested wetlands and marshes have in common?

How are forested wetlands and marshes different?

Mineral soil is made of small pieces of rock and minerals.

Organic soil is made of decomposing plant or animal matter.

Forested Wetland

Soil type: mineral

Dominant plant life: trees

Water source: fresh or salt water

Marsh

Soil type: mineral

Dominant plant life: grasses

Water source: fresh or salt water

How are marshes and fens similar?

How are bogs and fens different?

Bog

Soil type: organic

Dominant plant life: mosses

Water source: freshwater precipitation

Fen

Soil type: organic

Dominant plant life: grasses

Water source: fresh surface water and groundwater

What do bogs and fens have in common?

Bogs have little drainage. When the bog floods, excess water runs off along the ground.

Excess water in fens drains off into rivers or in the groundwater.

Find the Animal

Barred owls make a hooting sound that sounds like they are saying "Who cooks for you."

Beaver teeth are orange because they contain iron, which makes them stronger for cutting down trees.

Bobcats get their name from their naturally-short tails. "Bob" is an old-fashioned word that means "to cut short".

Flying squirrels can glide for distances over 150 feet.

Green darners will fly south for the winter, often in large swarms.

Snapping turtles eat both plants and animals (omnivores). One-third of their diet comes from plants.

Spring peeper bodies can freeze almost completely solid during the winter. They wake up in the spring when they warm up.

Wood ducks build nests in tree holes. Their ducklings can jump out of a nest from up to 50 feet in the air without hurting themselves.

Answers: A) green darner. B) barred owl. C) flying squirrel. D) beaver.
E) snapping turtle. F) wood duck. G) bobcat. H) spring peeper.

For my mom, who inspired me in so many ways.—KK

Thanks to Ellen Rondomanski, Lead Environmental Educator at Shangri La Botanical Gardens and Nature Center, for verifying the accuracy of the information in this book.

Library of Congress Cataloging-in-Publication Data

Names: Kurtz, Kevin, author. | Neidigh, Sherry, illustrator.
Title: A day in a forested wetland / by Kevin Kurtz ; illustrated by Sherry Neidigh.
Description: Mount Pleasant, SC : Arbordale Publishing, [2018] | Audience: Ages 4-8. | Audience: K to grade 3. | Includes bibliographical references.
Identifiers: LCCN 2018005024 (print) | LCCN 2018005586 (ebook) | ISBN 9781628559156 (English Downloadable eBook) | ISBN 9781628559170 (English Interactive Dual-Language eBook) | ISBN 9781628559163 (Spanish Downloadable eBook) | ISBN 9781628559187 (Spanish Interactive Dual-Language eBook) | ISBN 9781628559125 (english hardcover) | ISBN 9781628559132 (english pbk.) | ISBN 9781628559149 (spanish pbk.)
Subjects: LCSH: Forest animals--Juvenile literature. | Forest ecology--Juvenile literature. | Wetland ecology--Juvenile literature. | Forests and forestry--Juvenile literature.
Classification: LCC QL112 (ebook) | LCC QL112 .K865 2018 (print) | DDC 591.73--dc23
LC record available at https://lccn.loc.gov/2018005024

Bibliography:

Conner, Richard N, Clifford E. Shackleford, Daniel Saenz and Richard R. Schaefer. "Interactions Between Nesting Pileated Woodpeckers and Wood Ducks." Wilson Bulletin, 113(2), 2001.
Krautwurst, Terry. "When Squirrels Fly: From its Aerodynamics to its Ecodynamics, the Flying Squirrel is a Biological Marvel." Mother Earth News: June-July 2005.
Moore, Peter D. Wetlands. New York: Facts on File, 2001.
Muller-Schwarze, Dietland. *The Beaver: Its Life and Impact.* Ithaca: Comstock Pub. Associates, 2011.
Paulsen, Dennis R. *Dragonflies and Damselflies of the West.* Princeton: Princeton University Press, 2009.
Sibley, David. *The Sibley Guide to Bird Life and Behavior.* New York: Alfred A. Knopf, 2001.
Tiner, Ralph. *In Search of Swampland: A Wetland Sourcebook and Primer.* New Brunswick: Rutger University Press, 2005.
United States Department of Agriculture. "Biodiversity in Red Maple Forested Wetlands." June 2012.
Voshell, J. Reese. *A Guide to Common Invertebrates of North America.* Blacksburg: McDonald & Woodburg Publishing Co., 2002.

Animals in the book ilnclude: woodpecker, wood duck, green darner, mosquito, snapper turtle, caddisfly, spring peepers, bats, bobcat, diving beetle, flying squirrel, fishing spider, barred owl, beaver

Lexile® Level: 740L
key phrases: habitat, behavioral adaptations, physical adaptations, wetlands, forest, time of day, marsh, fen, bog

Printed in China, July 2018
This product conforms to CPSIA 2008
First Printing

Arbordale Publishing
Mt. Pleasant, SC 29464
www.ArbordalePublishing.com

Text Copyright 2018 © by Kevin Kurtz
Illustration Copyright 2018 © by Sherry Neidigh

The "For Creative Minds" educational section may be copied by the owner for personal use or by educators using copies in classroom settings